I0482576

Resume

The Secrets to Writing a Resume that is Guaranteed to Get You the Job

Table of Contents

Introduction

I want to thank you and congratulate you for purchasing the book, *Resume: The Secrets to Writing a Resume that is Guaranteed to Get You the Job.*

This book contains proven steps and strategies on how to craft effective resumes.

This Book will discuss the basic information related to resumes. It will explain the main purpose of a resume and how it can help you in securing job offers. With this eBook, you'll discover the major elements of a resume, the things recruiters look for when reviewing a resume, and how to create a resume that suits the job you're applying for. This material will also arm you with tips, tricks, techniques, and strategies that can make writing great resumes a walk in the park.

If you're looking for an in-depth guide about resume writing, this is the perfect book for you. Apply the ideas included in this book and you will have high chances of getting hired.

Thanks again for downloading this book, I hope you enjoy it!

Chapter 1: Writing a Resume – The Basics

In this chapter, you'll learn about the core concepts of resume writing. It will provide you with tips, tricks, techniques, and strategies that you can use in crafting a great resume.

The Objectives of Your Resume

Resumes are documents that allow you to present different information about you (e.g. your skills, work experience, etc.). You can use resumes for different purposes. In most cases, however, you'll use them for securing employment.

Effective resumes involve various elements, all of which apply, regardless if you're a fresh graduate or a seasoned executive. You'll learn about these elements later. For now, let's discuss the main objectives of a resume. These objectives are:

Attract the Reader's Attention

Your resume must attract and impress your readers (i.e. the HR personnel of the company you're applying to). Your chances of getting the job you want won't increase just because you love your resume. Rather, you should make sure that your actual readers will love the resume you're working on. That means you need to know your readers first before writing anything.

If the position you're applying for belongs to the "corporate" category, your resume must match it. For instance, use bullet points to present your achievements. Additionally, refrain from using decorative colors and/or fonts. The resume of an artist, however, can contain fancy elements since their readers are creative and artistic.

Important Note: While proofreading your work, ask yourself whether your resume matches the position you are applying for. If you are an HR executive, would you consider that as an effective resume?

Present Professionalism

During a hiring process, first impressions play a huge role. Consider this scenario: one of your friends told you that he would introduce you to someone. When that "someone" arrives, you immediately saw that there are ketchup stains on her shirt and skirt. Your brain will create assumptions about that person based on her appearance. You would think that you know what kind of person she is even before shaking her hand. This principle also applies to resumes.

If your resume has "ketchup stains" (e.g. typographical errors) on it, the hiring manager will instantly create assumptions, mostly negative ones, about you.

Important Note: Your resume should help you create a positive and professional first impression. With this kind of resume, you have excellent chances of getting the job of your dreams.

Highlight Your Skills and Achievements

Effective resumes present the applicant's skills and achievements relevant to the position he/she is applying for. Writing down what you can do (i.e. your skills, abilities, potential, etc.) and what you did (i.e. in your previous job) can be difficult. Most applicants focus on their actual tasks and responsibilities too much. However, this approach is ineffective. Instead of focusing on "I did this," you must concentrate on how your previous tasks and accomplishments helped your former employer.

Important Note: Always provide concrete examples to support each of your "achievement statements." This way, you can secure a competitive edge over other applicants.

Ten Things You Need to Know About Resumes

1. Recruiters want to know the skills and achievements you can offer. Don't focus on your previous duties; doing so will prevent you from catching the employer's attention. Remember, most applicants use that approach in writing resumes. If you want to be noticed, emphasize more on your achievements and provide examples of the things that you did for your previous company, if applicable.

2. Recruiters throw resumes away even if they haven't read half of the first page. There are many reasons for this behavior. The most common ones are poor grammar, bad spelling, fancy fonts, and long sentences.

3. The main objective of your resume is to help you get an interview. Don't treat your resume as an artistic masterpiece that you can hang on your living room wall. Refrain from including useless information in your resume. If your desired position requires decision-making skills, provide concrete examples of how you exhibited those skills in the past. State your examples clearly and concisely.

4. A resume that focuses on past achievements offers great chances of getting an interview.

5. Avoid the following mistakes:

    a) Spelling/Grammar Mistakes
    b) Irrelevant Data
    c) No Specific Dates
    d) "SMS Abbreviations" (e.g. "I will c 2 it that ur company...")
    e) Insufficient career highlights or achievements

6. A career summary (if written well) can boost the effectiveness of your resume. However, "generic" or

badly written summaries can hurt your chances of getting the job. Consider your career summary as a way to introduce yourself to the HR personnel. Thus, you need to provide valuable and specific information in your summary. Generic details (e.g. "loyal, goal-oriented person who has problem-solving skills") won't help you in the application process.

7. Addressing gaps (if any) in your work history can be extremely difficult. For example, if you spent one or more years performing community work, you might have some problems explaining it through your resume. Fortunately, a cover letter can help you in this matter. Use a cover letter to give detailed information about your hiatus.

8. You may add your hobbies and/or personal interests in your resume if they add more value to your application. Make sure that all of the details in your resume are relevant to the job you are applying for. If your hobby is irrelevant to the job, don't include it in your resume.

9. The length of your resume depends on the "career stage" you are in. If you have just graduated, your resume should have two pages. If you already have previous work experience, your resume may have three to four pages. However, according to hiring experts, the ideal length of a resume is two to three pages.

10. The positions you must include in your employment history will depend on your work experience. If you're a new graduate, you may include positions not closely related to the position you're applying for. This approach helps you inform the company that you have experienced working before, although not really in the industry they belong to. Senior applicants, on the other hand, may choose only the positions related to the job they want.

Writing a Resume for an Executive Position

If you want to get that "executive" position you've been dreaming about, you need to create a resume that emphasizes your skills, abilities, experience, and qualifications. You want to be an executive, so you must "show" your readers that you can perform all of the tasks and responsibilities related to the job. Additionally, the skills that you'll include in your resume should reflect your career goals and professional objectives.

Here are the things you need to do to create a great "executive resume":

1. Read the vacancy profile thoroughly and list down your career objectives. Obviously, your goals should align with the job you want.
2. Determine the skills, experiences, and abilities you have that match the available position.
3. Write down your experiences and qualifications. Then, choose the ones that are most suitable for the job.
4. Emphasize and explain your previous achievements and discuss how they helped your former employer/s. This way, you can highlight your capabilities as an executive.
5. List down your employment history, starting from your most recent job. Focus on how you attained the requirements of those positions (e.g. cost reduction, improved revenues, development of new products, etc.).
6. Include your educational background, particularly the ones related to the executive position. If you have completed leadership training or other courses before, add them to your resume.
7. Present the information clearly. Be consistent with your writing style while creating a resume.
8. Make sure that you don't put any irrelevant information in your executive resume. You are applying for an executive position, so the HR personnel will surely check your resume thoroughly. Thus, all of the details in your resume should help you in getting an interview.

These details should also show the HR people that you can help the company in reaching its goals.

9. Include some "power words" in your resume. These words can emphasize your skills, abilities and experience. Here are some of the power words that you can use:

   a) negotiation
   b) presentation
   c) business development
   d) employee development
   e) tactical planning
   f) team building
   g) customer retention
   h) coaching and mentoring
   i) lead generation

Chapter 2: Getting Your Dream Job Using Your Resume

This chapter will discuss the importance of your resume in getting your dream job. It will arm you with ideas and principles that can guide you in improving your resumes.

A Resume's Importance

While you are on a "job hunt," you consider your resume as one of your most important possessions; a tool that can help you find a great job. However, once you get hired, the value of your resume will decline significantly. It will become a useless piece of paper. That is, until you search for a new job in the future.

Recent studies have shown that most college students (about 90% of the total) don't know how to create effective resumes. Additionally, when asked to write a resume, these students didn't provide any achievement.

In the present world, resumes need more than just correct formats and structures: they also need to be "eye-friendly." Resumes need to be attractive and pleasing to read. Keep in mind that for each available position, there may be 150-200 applicants with the same skills and experience as you. Because of this fact, it's not surprising that applicants with wrong resumes don't get interviewed.

According to hiring experts, applicants fail not because they don't have the right knowledge and/or abilities. Rather, they fail because their resumes are ineffective.

Important Note: If you still can't write an effective resume even after reading this book, consider getting the services of a professional resume writer. This person can help you in emphasizing your strengths and portraying professionalism. Don't allow your writing skills to stop you from getting an excellent job.

How to Get Noticed

There are many applicants vying for a single position. Unfortunately, hiring managers don't have enough time to read resumes thoroughly. Because of this, they only spend up to thirty seconds scanning a resume before deciding whether to throw it away or continue reading. Here are the things hiring managers look at when scanning a resume:

Grammar and Spelling Mistakes

Hiring managers consider bad grammar and incorrect spelling as unforgivable sins. These "sins" tell potential employers that an applicant is reckless, incompetent, or lacks basic language skills. Most hiring managers stop reading a resume as soon as these sins show up.

Structure and Presentation

If a recruiter is looking at two resumes, his eyes will naturally focus on the one that has the better structure. Excellent structure gives a positive first impression. Recruiters will analyze your application positively, even if they haven't read your resume completely. If two applicants have the same skills and work experience, recruiters will choose the applicant whose resume is more pleasing to the eye.

Think of your resume as a presentation. That document will tell the recruiter or hiring manager that you are the best applicant for the position. Use your resume to show professional image. This way, you can set yourself apart from other applicants.

The One-Size-Fits-All Approach

These days, countless websites help applicants write their resumes. These websites offer pre-made templates; you just have to choose the template that matches the position you're applying for. This approach offers speed and convenience. However, you should be careful when using templates. The layout, formatting, and presentation of resumes change rapidly as years go by. The template you're looking at may be "out of fashion."

In addition, since more than one hundred people apply for the same position, your resume should stand out. By launching Google and downloading a template, you take the risk of utilizing a template that countless other people might have used before.

If you'll analyze it, you can't actually rely on a free template that is being offered online. You should write your resume based on your strengths, experiences and objectives. You also need to streamline the details you'll include so that they are closely related to the position you want to get.

Rate Your Resume

You need to verify the quality of your resume before submitting it to your future employer. Here are some questions that can help you determine your resume's effectiveness:

- Does your resume contain specific achievements?
- Does the information it contains flow smoothly? Will the reader understand your employment history easily?
- Did you provide supporting evidence for each of your achievements?
- Did you include your important skills, abilities and experience?
- Did you provide complete information (e.g. dates and positions) regarding your employment history?
- Did you use "power words" in your resume?
- Does your resume have appropriate length?
- Is it easy to read?

- Are the skills and accomplishments you included relevant to the position you're applying for?
- Did you use the right format and structure?

Convert each "yes" into one point. If you got seven to eight points, your resume has the chance of reaching the top twenty percent of the applicants. If you want to reach the top ten percent, however, you need to garner ten points from this exercise. Review your resume and make the necessary adjustments.

Improve Your Resume
In this part of the book, you'll find several tactics that you can use in improving your resume. Read this material carefully: it can help you secure a job offer.

1. Never Submit a "Blank" Resume

Constructing a resume is not easy, particularly if you don't have any work experience to include. Most students experience this problem, and they try to solve it using the wrong approaches. Students either search for positions that don't require resumes or submit resumes that has minimal content.

Everyone has knowledge and abilities. Your task is to identify your strengths and include them in your resume. For example, students may look at their courses and recent projects. Students can write about their courses as if these are previous job positions. You may list down the courses you've taken that are related to the position you're applying for. Then, enumerate the roles you've played and the achievements you've attained while taking the course.

Important Note: Most of the time, an applicant is qualified for the job he/she is applying for. The problem lies in converting the applicant's skills, knowledge, and experience into words that attract recruiters and hiring managers.

2. Enhance Your Chances of Getting Hired While Studying

Often, students experience a hard time in getting hired. These people have similar skills and abilities, which makes it difficult to get noticed. Writing a great resume can certainly give you an advantage, but you should also do some things to increase your chances of getting hired.

New graduates lack experience. Employers are aware of this, so you don't have to worry about this aspect of your application. However, employers also know that students have access to countless opportunities for gaining experience. Students who utilize these opportunities often stand out in the hiring process.

There are a lot of resources and opportunities available to you. For example, organizations and businesses offer internship programs to students. Internships can help you gain valuable work experience. Additionally, an internship program is typically designed so that it has minimal effects on the intern's school work. The main disadvantage of this approach is that internships are usually unpaid.

Important Note: Working without pay is certainly not exciting. However, it can help you secure competitive advantages over other applicants once you earn your college diploma. You can never go wrong by gaining work experience.

3. Experience vs. Education

Many people encounter problems regarding the format of their resumes. These people can't decide which element they should list first: work experience or educational background. Just like most resume-related concerns, the answer depends on your situation.

Individuals who lack work experience (e.g. new graduates) usually list their education-related information first. According to employers, this is an effective approach when writing an entry-level applicant's resume. Education is always a good thing, so people who don't have any work experience can write about their education in the first part of their resumes. List down all of the academic awards you've obtained while in school (if any).

If your experience is more "colorful" than your education, on the other hand, you may write down your employment history first. You should also consider the position you're applying for. If you're applying for an executive position, for instance, highlighting your employment history is an excellent decision.

Important Note: Experience and education have equal importance. If you are confident with your experience and education, you can list either of them first. Then, include these two in your career summary. This way, the recruiter will immediately see them.

4. Use Power Words

With power words, you can double your chances of grabbing the hiring manager's attention. If you'll use cliché phrases (e.g. excellent team player) in your resume, the recruiter will likely ignore your application. People involved in the hiring process hate "canned" words and statements. Power words, on the other hand, inspire recruiters to continue reading one's resume.

Here are the power words that you can include in your resume:

helped, financed, secured, taught, balanced, designed, observed, attained, quoted, delegated, detected, closed, comply, provided, programmed, scheduled, collaborated, maintained, justified, recovered, reinstated, sustained, triumphed

5. Add Your Major Achievements

As an applicant, your goal is to show how you can help the company. Promises of future excellence aren't enough. You need to show your capabilities by listing down your past behaviors and successes.

You should include the following in your resume:

- The times you helped your previous employer save company resources
- The times you generated and/or executed ideas that led to positive results
- The recognitions and special awards you have received
- Hiring, leading, training, and mentoring employees
- The problems and/or issues you solved successfully
- The courses, workshops, and seminars you've attended

6. Focus on Numbers

Effective resumes contain quantitative evidence. This kind of detail emphasizes your accomplishments and presents them in an easy-to-understand form. If your previous job involved product development, for instance, you shouldn't use a generic statement (e.g. Creative leader). Rather, you need to provide a statement that explains your accomplishment. Here are some examples:

Sample 1: Effective product development and management helped the company to exceed annual targets by 20%.

Sample 2: Led a group of eight product specialists in generating new ideas and developing new products. This management resulted to an increase in revenue amounting to $3 million within one year.

Sample 3: Member of a product development team who launched three new products in one year. This led to a 20% increase in profits.

Chapter 3: The Mistakes You Should Avoid

In this part of the book, you'll discover the fatal blunders committed by inexperienced "resume writers." Read this material carefully if you want to create a flawless resume: a tool that can help you secure a job offer.

First Mistake – Never Underestimate Your Work Experience

Most college students and entry-level applicants don't include temporary and/or part-time jobs in their resumes. Many students have worked in a business involved in hospitality or retail. However, these students don't include their work experience since the positions they held were "not real" and/or "part-time only." If you'll ask a student regarding this behavior, you'll probably get a response similar to this: "How can that work experience improve my resume?"

Actually, most temporary and/or part-time positions that students hold offer knowledge, skills, and experience – the stuff recruiters are searching for. These recruiters know that students and fresh graduates lack work experience. Thus, they treat any form of work experience as an applicant's competitive advantage.

The secret here lies in stating your experience effectively. If you have worked in a retail store, don't say that you "completed transactions" or "placed goods in recyclable bags." Rather, state that you reached (or even exceeded) the sales targets assigned to you or that you have maintained solid relationships with the company's customers.

Second Mistake – Attaching a Bad Photo to Your Resume

In some countries, employers prefer resumes that have the

applicant's photo. Here, you need to make sure that your photo exudes professionalism. Keep in mind that you want to get hired. You may look awesome without your shirt on, but please don't add a shirtless selfie onto your resume. It's better to submit a photo-free resume than a resume that has a scandalous image.

Third Mistake – Failure to Submit a Cover Letter

People who fail to submit a cover letter have extremely low chances of getting hired. If you didn't prepare a cover letter, recruiters will think that you didn't exert additional effort for your application. Many recruiters ignore applicants that don't have a cover letter.

Fourth Mistake – Providing Vague Details Regarding Your Employment History

If you will add work experience in your resume, be specific as much as you can. Work experience is an important part of your application, so don't make your potential employer guess what you did in your previous job. Listing job titles in your resume doesn't work. If you won't provide specific information regarding your previous job, don't mention that job in your resume.

Fifth Mistake – Using Too Much Words

Long-winded resumes are extremely boring. Recruiters are usually impatient when it comes to long and wordy resumes. This is easy to understand: recruiters need to read hundreds of resumes in order to find the best applicants. If your resume contains excessive words, the recruiter will likely frown and look at your document with distaste. Remember: extra words are not equivalent to extra points.

Sixth Mistake – Using Negative Statements

Negativity has no place in the application process. Forget

about the negative stuff while writing your resume (and while answering the recruiter's questions during an interview). Keep the negative stuff to yourself. Remember that your resume's goal is to "sell" you. Recruiters don't need to know that your previous boss is an ungrateful, perfectionist, and hard-headed moron. Don't even try to discuss it in your resume: explaining this kind of topic on paper can lead to disasters.

Seventh Mistake – Using Highfalutin Words

Naturally, you would like to impress the people who will read your resume. There are a lot of things you can do to achieve this goal. However, using highfalutin words isn't one of them. Using rare words (e.g. honestation, hufty-tufty, hesitude, etc.) doesn't help in presenting yourself smartly and professionally.

Chapter 4: Tailor-fit Your Resume

In this part of the book, you'll learn how to tailor your resume so that it matches the position you're applying for. By applying the tips and techniques discussed here, your resume will have better chances of securing interviews and job offers.

The Fundamentals

Your resume should indicate your knowledge, abilities, and work experience. Since these things are constant, your resumes will certainly look the same. However, it would be a huge mistake if you won't even try to customize your resumes for the specific positions you're applying for. If you want recruiters to interview you, you need to show them how your strengths match the particular job you are interested in.

While customizing your resume, the part that you should focus on is the description of the available position. Here are some tips that can help you in this regard:

Customize Your Preferred Job Title

Many job descriptions provide specific details (e.g. job titles, required skills, etc.). It would be best if the job title that you'll write on your resume matches the one on the advertisement. Place this title in the upper section of your resume. This way, the recruiter can easily determine whether your application must be considered or not.

Choose the Right Order When Listing Your Skills

After writing the job title, you need to identify the crucial requirements for the position. You also need to determine the best arrangement for the skills that you'll include. Most applicants place their work experience in the first section of their resume. However, there are no specific rules regarding this. If you want to place other parts (e.g. your education) first, you may do so. You just have to make sure that your chosen arrangement makes sense and allows easy reading.

Be Mindful of Your Language

The easiest way to customize your resume is by using words that match the responsibilities listed in the advertisement. You can take this technique a step further by learning more about the company. Discover the company's vision, mission and core values. With this approach, you can instill the right "personality" into your resume. You can make recruiters feel that you belong to their company.

Tell Them the Reason Behind Your Application

Recruiters should be able to tell, in just one reading, the main reason/s why you want to work for their company. They should also know the contributions that you can make if you will get hired.

The Time-Tested Guidelines for Crafting Tailored Resumes

- Start your resume with an objective. For instance, you may write, "Accountant for Omega Inc." Make sure that the remaining sections of your resume match your chosen objective.
- If you will summarize your qualifications, make sure that they are specific and related to your objective.
- Place the important details in the first half of your resume's first page. This approach makes sure that the recruiter will see the highlights of your application quickly.
- Don't just list your previous job titles and responsibilities. Add some excitement into your resume by citing your previous contributions and accomplishments.
- Drop some names. If your previous job allowed you to work with reputable clients, mention their names. If

your position covered different states, name those states one by one. This will improve the authenticity and specificity of your resume.

- Use paragraphs of different lengths. If all of the paragraphs in your resume have four to five sentences, the recruiter will surely have some problems reading through it. It's important to change the length of your paragraphs. In many cases, one to two sentences are enough to state a point.

Chapter 5: What Does A Recruiter Look For?

This chapter will focus on the things a recruiter looks for while reading a resume. If you know what your readers want to see, writing effective resumes will become easy and simple.

The Style

- Many recruiters don't appreciate photos and personal data (e.g. religion). Additionally, these people don't like tables, shading, boxes, and templates.
- Recruiters look for consistency in terms of spacing, font style, and font size.
- Recruiters prefer fonts that can be read easily. Some of the best fonts for resume writing are Calibri, Garamond, Tahoma, and Times New Roman.
- The margins of your resume should be limited to .5 to 1 inch. The size that you should choose relies on the space available to you.
- Most recruiters love bullet points. This kind of list allows easy presentation of valuable data. Thus, convert your long paragraphs into bullet points whenever possible.
- Make sure that the paper used for your resume has a professional color (e.g. white or light-grey).
- Recruiters look for professional email addresses (e.g. yourname@yourschoolemail.com). Don't use personal email addresses (e.g. potatofries999@samplesite.com, wetandwild@samplesite.com, smellybelly1@samplesite.com, etc.) for your application.

The Content

- Your statements should be focused, concise and straightforward. The information you'll include should help you sell yourself. Don't use personal pronouns (e.g.

me).

- Recruiters expect your resume to contain certain parts such as skills, education, work experience, and professional summary.
- PhD applicants who are going for R&D positions must list their previous conferences, publications and presentations. If you don't want your resume to be too academic, you may use the term "project" when referring to your dissertation.
- Add numbers into your achievements whenever you can.
- Recruiters expect your resume to be one to two pages long. If your resume has three or more pages, recruiters might think that you included unnecessary details.
- If the position you're applying for has more connection with your education than your work experience, write down your education first.

Your Experience

- Use different sources (e.g. school projects, researches, presentations, volunteer work, etc.) while working on your work experience and past achievements. Keep in mind that fresh graduates can use their undergraduate years in lieu of actual employment history.
- You don't have to list down all of the jobs you've had before. However, it would be best if you'll record all the relevant details of your employment history. This way, you can easily access, copy, and paste the work experience that suits the position you're applying for.
- Don't treat your resume as an autobiography. Filter the information you'll include: focus on the details that your potential employer needs to know.
- Divide your work experience into different headings. This approach will help the recruiter in reviewing your employment history.
- You may also divide your work experience into two major groups: (1) related and (2) additional.

Conclusion

Thank you again for purchasing this book!

I hope this book was able to help you write resumes that can secure interviews and job offers.

The next step is to find job ads that are related to your current skills and work experience. Read the ads thoroughly and plan your resume in advance. Focus on the details that the recruiter needs to know. With a focused, detailed, and tailor-made resume, your chances of getting hired will soar to new heights.

Finally, if you enjoyed this book, then I'd like to ask you for a favor, would you be kind enough to leave a review for this book on Amazon? It'd be greatly appreciated!

Thank you and good luck!

www.ingramcontent.com/pod-product-compliance
Lightning Source LLC
Chambersburg PA
CBHW070308190526
45169CB00004B/1547